111 PIECES OF ~~MY~~ YOUR HOME

MUSKAN AGRAWAL

INDIA • SINGAPORE • MALAYSIA

ISBN 979-8-89277-803-9

to my lovelies, a piece of my heart

WAY FORWARD

This book is divided into four seasons, and each season is the replica of an emotion: how winters freeze all our brains and hearts and make us cold and, on the other hand, how spring showers positivity but still we wait for the summer to reach our end goal, but as summer comes, rainy season awaits. It means we will always have rainbows, but not without rain; it's a sign of moving forward no matter what. I hope this book serves you well!

RAIN

– 1 –

I have a lot to say, but I am not able to frame it in words!

– 2 –

I always wanted to be understood and ended up being misunderstood!

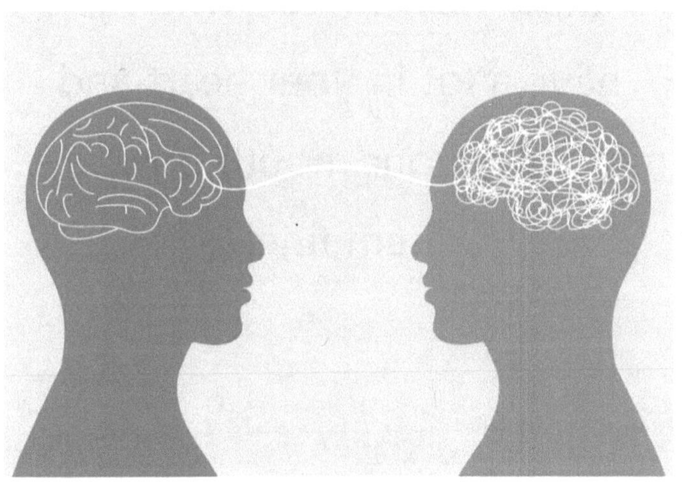

– 3 –

I know how it feels when you have a lot in your heart and mind, but your mouth only says, "I am fine!"

– 4 –

Please stop it, you are overthinking, I have heard this a lot of times, I wish I could tell them no one wants to put themselves in pain.

– 5 –

All this time, I wanted and tried a lot for them to be apart because I was scared I would be left alone.

– 6 –

I tried sorting it out with
everyone and ended up
feeling lonely.

– 7 –

Sometimes. I feel this loneliness
this void will eat me.

– 8 –

I want to be saved; I just don't know how.

– 9 –

Most of the time, I cry in silence, waiting for the day my pain will turn into power.

– 10 –

Whom do you want to be saved from? I replied, "Myself."

– 11 –

They say I have depth in my thoughts, I wish they can see deep thoughts only come from people who have suffered or suffering from deep pain.

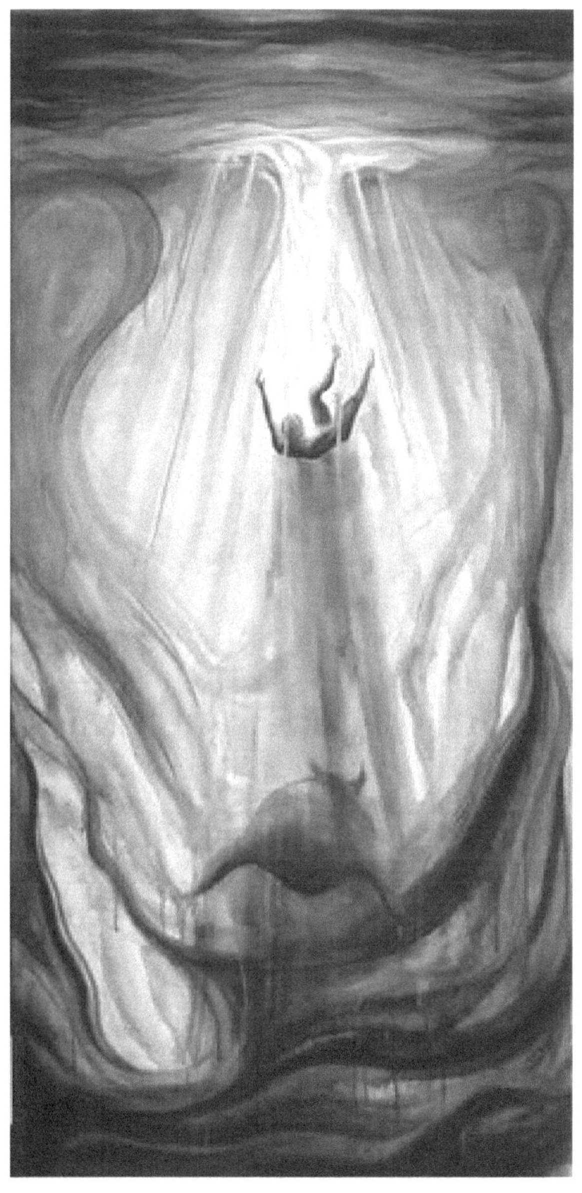

– 12 –

All these panic attacks, all those tears, all those shivering, makes you believe you are not made for anything good, and that's the battle we have to win.

– 13 –

Never let anyone treat you so badly that you start feeling this is what you deserve.

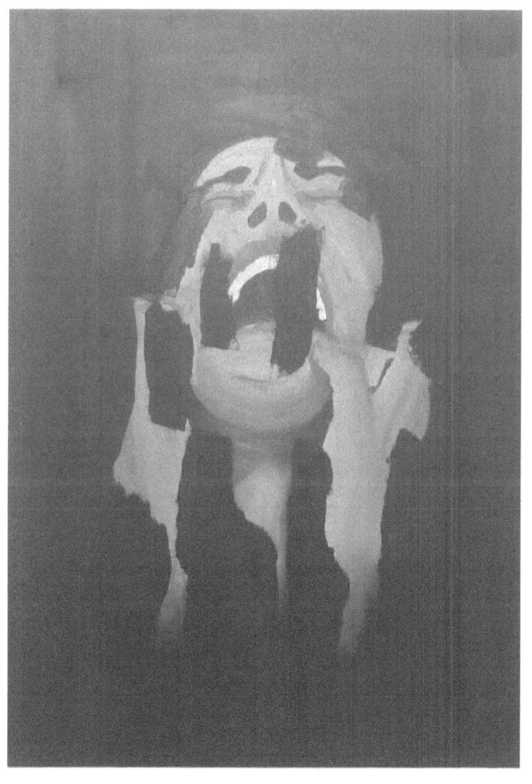

– 14 –

All this time, I was trying very hard to make people love me the way I deserve!

– 15 –

No one can understand your pain, but they will surely expect from you to understand theirs.

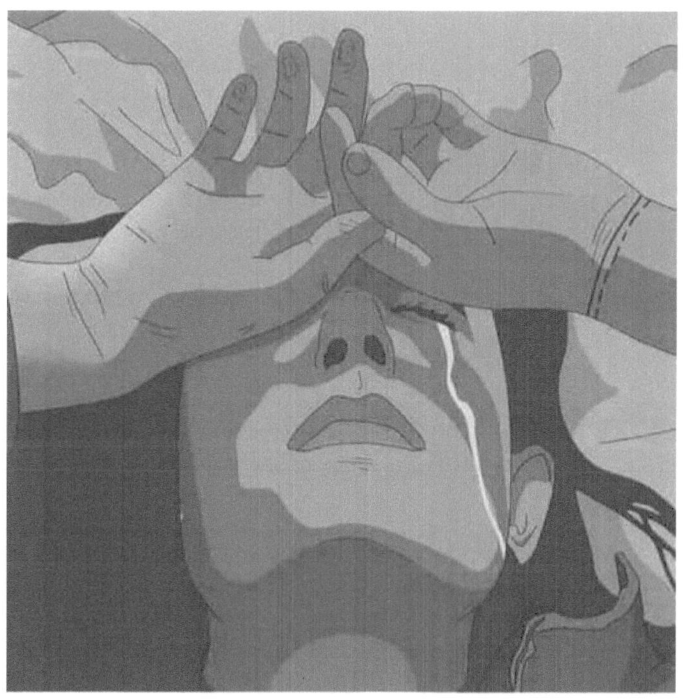

WINTER

– 16 –

I wish I could look at myself differently, not in the way my mind wants it to be, but in the way my gut wants it to be.

– 17 –

I have enough people around me, but still there is a void in my heart that is waiting for someone to be filled with.

– 18 –

I don't regret any of my relationships because they have taught me a lot, so why do I regret the relationship I have with myself? These are the questions that kept arising every day.

– 19 –

I have seen people changing
more than seasons.

– 20 –

I am sure one day you will look back and miss whatever you have now if you don't stop living in the past.

– 21 –

I am in a constant dilemma

about whether he loves

me or not.

– 22 –

I want to pen down every emotion I have, but my mind is stuck somewhere else.

– 23 –

This world has made me so confused that I don't know who I am anymore.

– 24 –

How to decide who is best for me when I can't even decide what is best for me

– 25 –

No matter how much you try, if you don't work on your inside, you are going to fall again and again.

– 26 –

The most painful thing you can give to yourself is to look for validation.

– 27 –

As each day was passing, life was getting more difficult, I had no clue what to even sort now.

– 28 –

It's okay to cry, but it's not okay to suffer in pain.

– 29 –

You are alone, and that is not a bad thing unless you don't feel lonely.

– 30 –

I always looked myself down if they used to treat me badly, not realising their behaviour was not related to my self-worth.

– 31 –

I was always confused between what was right and what I was feeling.

– 32 –

Society is so fucked up that you are left with two choices- either be the society or create a society of your own.

SPRING

– 33 –

I have heard that no one is going to save you, you can only save yourself but still my heart is aching for someone as if it knows who can save it.

– 34 –

I always believed in the story
that my grandma used to read
it to me about how a princess is
saved only by the prince!

– 35 –

And every day, I was passing in the hope that maybe people would change, and trust me, it's one of the most terrible situations you can put yourself into!

– 36 –

Scrolling social media and looking for the signs made me believe in hope again!

– 37 –

We all have gone through something that made us want to give up, but here we are, thinking we won't survive this.

– 38 –

It's okay to feel you are the only one who is going through this but trust me, one day; you will realise you weren't alone.

– 39 –

I really hope you find the courage to believe in your gut, and to trust yourself back again.

– 40 –

It's the day I realised I was fighting for the position in their life not for the bond.

– 41 –

You can speak whatever you want with your heart and mind, but what if they still don't understand?

– 42 –

I wish I never got acquainted with the truth; sometimes, it is peaceful not knowing about it.

– 43 –

I wish you could look me the way I look at you.

– 44 –

Some mornings make me feel not to wake up again, but then the alarm rings(romance).

– 45 –

Every day, I want to remind myself that I should focus on people who love me instead of people who don't!

– 46 –

Hanging out with the wrong kind of people can make you doubt yourself.

– 47 –

I realised I needed validation because I didn't feel worthy enough, and that hit me hard.

– 48 –

I know you must be feeling why you have to go through all this or why this is only happening to you, but the game will change when, instead of asking the reason, you will start changing the situation.

– 49 –

You can re-write your life as much as you want.

– 50 –

I know life gets tough in such a way that you don't know how to get back on track, but you have to keep going as you are made for bigger things.

– 51 –

It all starts at home! (doesn't matter the good or the bad).

– 52 –

No matter what you do, how much you do for them, the one who has a habit of finding faults will always do the same!

– 53 –

If you ever doubt your worth,
look at how far you have come.

– 54 –

Never compare others' success with yours; everyone has their own battle.

– 55 –

I hate comparison, but you are a better human being if you have not taken advantage of someone else situation.

– 56 –

To stop revolving in the same situation, you need to find the reason for the void in your heart.

– 57 –

After all the loneliness I have felt,

my heart wants peace.

– 58 –

Who are you when no one is looking at you?

– 59 –

Whenever you get confused or feel stuck, just ask yourself who are you, the real you.

SUMMER

– 60 –

You don't realise how small things can affect someone in a good or bad way, until you get affected by one.

– 61 –

I will never forget the words that touched my heart. Whether it is good or bad, I might accept it, but I will always have it with me.

– 62 –

After comparing my healing to everyone's healing, here I am writing about my healing.

– 63 –

I don't know if you relate to me,

but I feel related to you!

– 64 –

The greatest gift I ever gave to myself was accepting that one day, everything will be fine, and rain is always followed by the sun.

– 65 –

One day, I realised to ache for a prince, you need to be a princess who can survive on her own.

– 66 –

I know you feel your stars and angels are not with you, but I have seen my angels protecting me in so many situations where I couldn't take care of myself.

– 67 –

You can change your destiny and your stars if you have one thing with you ‘belief.’

– 68 –

I don't want to be dependent on anyone except for the one who never tries to steal my independence.

– 69 –

All this time, I thought I was scared of losing something, but now that something has a term 'freedom.'

– 70 –

One day, you will stop expecting, and trust me, that will be the day you will be winning.

– 71 –

Sending you ~~sunflower~~ to your favourite flower; that's how I learned to love them the way they want, not in the way I want.

– 72 –

Kind people never make you count what they have done for you.

– 73 –

The person who blames you for covering their mistake is a big type of red flag.

– 74 –

It's hard to believe people if you don't believe yourself, read that again.

– 75 –

In this dynamic environment, your dreams, goals, and aspirations will never leave you.

– 76 –

To understand someone, you need to put aside your habit of replying to whatever they are saying; not everyone needs advisers, some need listeners.

– 77 –

Love is as deep as the ocean, troubles in a relationship are like waves in an ocean; you can't run from it; you just have to accept it as a part of your relationship.

– 78 –

After chasing everyone, here I am, convincing myself to accept that I deserve better.

– 79 –

I know it sounds unacceptable, but living alone is better than chasing someone who doesn't want to be chased.

– 80 –

Some things need to be sorted out; some things need to be left out.

– 81 –

I realised that my biggest enemy
was no one but me.

– 82 –

People will say,

“don't overthink it,”

“You are overthinking, it will be fine.”

Remember, they are not in your

situation; you do you!

– 83 –

If you want peace in your life, focus on what is important to you rather than focusing on everything!

– 84 –

We all go through something that makes us realise how to behave and react when someone goes through the same.

– 85 –

I get hurt every day trying to be the best for them so that they like me, but not anymore!

– 86 –

I am done looking for validation so that I can feel my worth.

– 87 –

I need to remind myself every day that no matter what they do, what they say, whom they like, it is not related to my self-worth.

– 88 –

Helping someone without having any expectations will give you peace.

– 89 –

One of the pieces of advice I would like to give you is to fear no one and fear nothing.

– 90 –

I realised I am made to be free, not to be trapped, be it free from my thoughts or any boundaries.

– 91 –

Never take any financial help from someone if you have the capability to do it by yourself.

– 92 –

If you aren't able to fulfil your small goals, how will you fulfil your big goals?

– 93 –

Trust me, once you start working on yourself, be it achieving small goals, you are making a big change for yourself in the long term.

– 94 –

Communication will only solve your problem; speak it or end it.

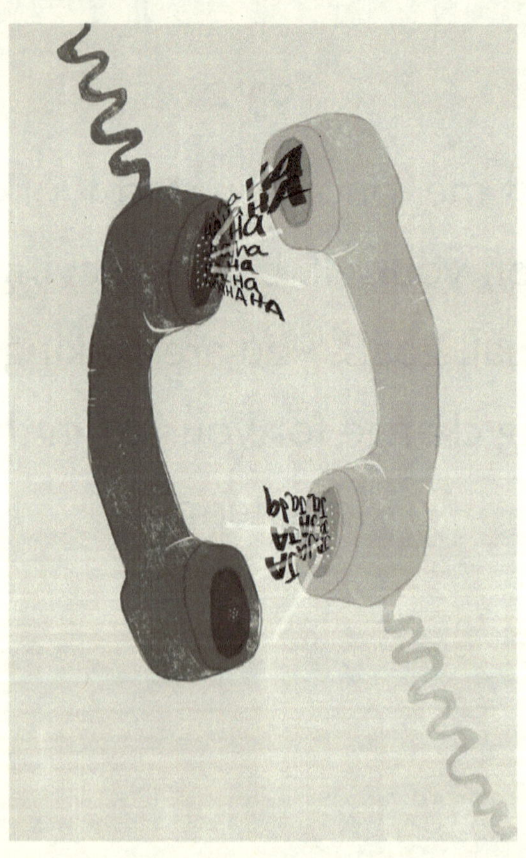

– 95 –

Crying can help you in releasing anger, make you feel lighter, give you clarity, glow your skin, then why people say crying shows weakness?

– 96 –

Loneliness is a state where one should not work on their environment but on themselves.

– 97 –

Stand up for yourself, no matter against whom you have to take a stand for.'

– 98 –

You have survived those parts where most of the people failed.

– 99 –

Don't let the outer world change your good intentions; I repeat, don't let them change your good intentions.

– 100 –

Never forget what they have done for you and what they have done to you.

– 101 –

This world already has a lot of hate to give; please start giving love!

SPREAD THE LOVE

– 102 –

It's so easy to blame your parents or anyone, but hard to act differently from them.

– 103 –

All this time, while you are blaming someone for blaming you, take a pause and look at yourself; you are exactly doing the same.

– 104 –

Life changed when I started thanking God for everything instead of asking him for everything.

– 105 –

Taking a trip can make you learn so many things that you can't even imagine .

– 106 –

If you can't do it by yourself, no one is going to do it for you.

– 107 –

Don't make anger your basic part of nature.

– 108 –

Truth needs no noise.

– 109 –

I won't suggest you to be like water, as sometimes you lose yourself in the process. Instead, I'll ask you to be like oil, which never loses it's identity, even if we mix it with water.

– 110 –

As you grow, you realise no matter how hard you try, you cannot change anyone's attitude or feelings towards you until they want to.

– 111 –

And whenever life puts you in a situation, remember there are angels protecting you (11:11)

REFERENCE

2. Rain
sourced from Pinterest
@ Kasia ciszewski

4. Rain
sourced from Pinterest
@ Vecteezy.com

7 rain
sourced from Pinterest
@ At.tumblr.com

10 rain
sourced from Pinterest
@ Commarts.com

11 rain
sourced from Pinterest
@ Boredpanda.com

13 rain
sourced from Pinterest
@ Etsy.com

15 rain
sourced from Pinterest
@ https://in.pinterest.com/aaortee/

Winter 1
sourced from Pinterest
@ Iamzaynab13

Winter 2
sourced from Pinterest
@ Vicsxoo

Winter 6.
sourced from Pinterest
@ Iremdemir7

Winter 8
sourced from Pinterest
@ drawingart_ros

Winter 10
sourced from Pinterest
@ Homesthetics.net

Winter 13
No https://pin.it/2jnxjwcat

Spring 1
https://pin.it/fnkd6tr0j

Spring 5
sourced from Pinterest
@ Giannikachristina

Spring 8
sourced from Pinterest
@ Shaneh2a

Spring 11
sourced from Pinterest
@ Saatchiart.com

Spring14
sourced from instagram
@ Marina parras on instagram

Spring 17
sourced from Pinterest
@ Tiny j. White

Spring 19
sourced from Pinterest
@ Dovechristiancounseling.com

Spring 22
sourced from Pinterest
@ Shams allami

Spring 26
sourced from Pinterest
@ Artz now

Summer 3
sourced from Pinterest
@ Discover.hubpages.com

Summer 5
sourced from Pinterest
@ Windautumn

Summer 10
sourced from Pinterest
@ Anthony schultz

Summer 12
sourced from Pinterest
@ Saatchiart.com

Summer 16
sourced from Pinterest
@ Art by divya

Summer 20
sourced from Pinterest
@ https://pin.it/1fhjkrbun

Summer 24
sourced from Pinterest
@ https://pin.it/4jki9v1lt

Summer 27
sourced from Pinterest
@ Themindsjournal.com

Summer 30
sourced from Pinterest @ Bluesssatan.gumroad.com

Summer 35
sourced from Pinterest
@ Behance.net

Summer 39
sourced from Pinterest
@ Boredpanda.com

Summer 42
sourced from Pinterest
@ Redbubble.com

Summer 46
sourced from Pinterest
@ Dbutton0216

Summer 52
sourced from Pinterest
@ https://pin.it/4oB2V7b8q

ABOUT THE BOOK, FROM THE AUTHOR'S HEART

Thank you for being here. I believe after reading each quote, you must have questioned yourself and related it in your own way. Some answers must have been found, while others still need to be found! That's life to you; it's full of surprises, heartbreaks, and a circle of questions that make us feel whether we are doing right or not, but whenever you feel something like this, I want you to remember that you are always healing, you are always moving into a better place, even if you don't feel like it, and more importantly, you are getting close to whatever or whoever you want to be in the future!

And whenever you doubt yourself, you can always come to this book or to me through my email, @musuagrawal123@gmail.com.

ABOUT THE AUTHOR

Muskan, the meaning of the name, is to never stop smiling, and that is how she yearned to be, to never stop smiling even in situations you cannot process in the right manner. She was someone who was into spirituality, so she learned numerology, and while preparing for her civil services, she realised how everyone could have so many questions about themselves and the situations present in their life, and it is quite possible that they are not able to confront it to someone or even to themselves, so she tried putting her thoughts in a book with a hope that her book might work as a healer for those who are confused about their healing and an attempt for those who want to start healing, she has also written this book in memory of her grandmother after she passed her emotions have never been constant, it's all seasons only, but she never stop looking for summer.

www.ingramcontent.com/pod-product-compliance
Lightning Source LLC
LaVergne TN
LVHW091059150826
845673LV00002B/653

* 9 7 9 8 8 9 2 7 7 8 0 3 9 *